PEARLS

of

WISDOM

Dadi Janki

Health Communications, Inc.
Deerfield Beach, Florida

www.hci-online.com

D1275515

Library of Congress Cataloging-in-Publication Data

Dadi Janki
    Pearls of Wisdom
      p.   cm.
   ISBN 1-55874-723-0 (pbk.)
1. Spiritual Life.   Quotations, Maxims, etc. I. Title.
   BL 1237 .36
   294.5'432—dc21   99-29272
                                                    CIP

©1999 Brahma Kumaris Information Services

ISBN 1-55874-723-0

Publisher: Health Communications, Inc.
              3201 S.W. 15th Street
              Deerfield Beach, FL 33442-8190

Cover design by Andrea Brower
Inside book design by Dawn Grove

Contents

Introduction vii

Character 1

Life 39

Spirit 79

About the Author 121

About the Brahma Kumaris 123

Introduction

The gems in this little book derive from the practice of Raja Yoga, as taught by the Brahma Kumaris World Spiritual University.

Each pearl of wisdom has been mined from rich seams of experience. We hope that by reflecting upon and praticing each gem, you will enrich your life every day.

Other publications by the Brahma Kumaris include Companion of God, Inner Beauty, and Wings of Soul published by Health Communications, Inc.

Self-respect is not a matter of what you are doing in your life, but rather of how you are doing it. It requires that you bring quality and virtue into each action, whatever that action may be.

Sometimes you must burrow to find the good qualities in your nature that have gone underground and then coax them to the surface. Stopping for a moment and being silent can bring the steadiness you need for this task.

When discipline comes from commitment to a spiritual goal, it brings safety. It allows you to go on, to keep walking through the actions which will ultimately bring back your joy.

Keep your face toward the sun and you will not be bothered by shadows.

When your mind creates upheaval, practice self-governance. As you learn to rule your own thoughts with patience and kindness, they will better serve your aims.

In the midst of uncertainty, keep determination in your thoughts and it will become a guiding light in front of you.

Those whose thoughts are filled with determination find everything to be possible.

possible.

Battering at life from the outside, trying to change only what is visible, is inverted determination. When a quality of mind—peace, happiness, depth, purity—can remain still and uninterrupted by the bumps of life, that is true determination.

Determination leaves no gap between thought and action.

Your thoughts create your feelings. To save yourself from useless and painful feelings, don't think about useless or negative things.

If you want to change your behavior, focus on the thinking which causes it. Thoughts are like seeds. From them grow your attitudes and, in turn, your actions.

When you build a house, every brick counts. When you build character, every thought counts. So think constructively.

A humble person dismisses nothing, recognizing that whatever life presents needs to be respected. Inside even the smallest things there is often enormity.

Being humble does not require you to give of yourself indiscriminately. Have the wisdom to know the value of your inner resources and to give accordingly.

Honesty is most powerful when it involves not simply speaking your mind but being true to the best that is within you.

Flexibility means being able to make problems into teachers.

Just as you should never seek to control anyone, never allow anyone to control you. As important as not <u>giving</u> sorrow to anyone is not <u>taking</u> sorrow from anyone.

When one will not quarrel, two cannot.

Calmness and tolerance act like air conditioning in a hot room. They increase everyone's efficiency.

When you're shown disregard, check yourself. If you've done nothing wrong, and your attitude is well-meaning, understand the situation as a test of your ability to remain beyond the judgment of others.

Respect for another means offering criticism only where there is the strength to withstand it.

People will naturally start trusting you when they see you dealing with situations in a reliable and consistent way. An even more powerful way to gain the trust of others is to let them feel your trust in them.

To be of real help without taking root in someone else's mind requires great gentleness. See and understand without either willfully interfering or creating dependence.

Gentleness is not lack of strength but a quality which doesn't disturb, doesn't push, yet knows its own power.

Sweetness is a virtue that searches for the good in every person and situation. At its heart is the conviction that there is always something positive to be found. You simply need to have the patience to discover it.

When you notice weakness in another, aim instead to recognize a strength. The awareness that everyone has value will allow you to shift your focus.

Find at least one good quality in everyone, no matter how many defects are visible to you. The more you focus on the good, the more power you give to people and the sooner they will be able to change.

Mercy is the quality that sees the inner need behind expression. It looks behind anger and sees the sadness; behind coldness, the fear.

Detachment is being close to what you most want to be free from and using it to make you grow.

*O*bserving what is wrong, if done
with humility, can point the way
toward something right.

Not repeating your mistakes is a form of progress.

Self-confidence is to know your way around yourself so instinctively that you always have a strength to draw on. Somewhere inside, from the stillness, you can always find something to meet your need.

The process of self-transformation is not a 10-yard dash, but a 150-mile run. Patience makes the journey possible. It keeps you cool and calm. So pace yourself.

Being cooperative requires invisibility and precision. Help without splashing your name on the achievement, and leave without waiting for the results.

If you don't love a task 100 percent, somewhere underneath all the hard work will be a little cry for praise. Humility sees only what is good for the task itself.

If you have every virtue except humility, you will be a virtuous person who is arrogant about your virtues.

Approach each second with respect. If you move too fast, you miss the meeting point between mind and matter and become like the hare who scampered but lost the race.

Every moment has benefit, if only you know how to see it.

Integrity is a matter of considering the consequences of every action and of never being drawn mindlessly into anything.

The moment you live something, you are teaching it whether you want to or not.

Learning and teaching are players in the same game. If either one stops, everything becomes heavy and ceases to be fun. Learning is the reward for respecting life and teaching is the fruit of experiencing life.

Teaching others is best done with love. Once the heart has understood, the mind opens.

There will always be the opportunity to learn for those who desire it.

Developing an awareness of life beyond your immediate surroundings brings a healthy restlessness which, if infused with peace and used well, can be a foundation for positive change in the world.

Problems are challenges waiting for creative
solutions to meet them.

*C*rying over one opportunity missed can cloud the vision you need in order not to miss the next one.

The trick to problem solving is to get to the root of the problem before the rest of it shows up.

Illness is a chance to teach the mind to remain independent of physical circumstances and thus to connect with our inner resources. Experiencing these qualities is a powerful medicine.

Hope, enthusiasm and wisdom are to the mind as food is to the body. Everyone needs daily sustenance.

There are two aspects of life worth paying attention to. One is our actions; the other is the space in between our actions.

To observe your thoughts is the first step in understanding them and, ultimately, taking charge of them.

Wrestling with your mind weakens you.
When negative thoughts grab hold of you,
observe them without judgment and they will
loosen their grip.

To remain cheerful, learn how to cordon off areas of weakness. Once you refuse them entry into the rest of your mind, they can no longer influence you. Then you can work on them safely.

The first step toward conquering stress is to accept that it is not created by external events so much as by how we deal with them.

Even when there is nothing visible to be done in the face of a problem, the world still needs the support of tranquil minds.

There is no need to prove the truth. Trying to do so shows only your own stubbornness. Truth will always reveal itself at the right moment and the right place. You need be concerned only with living true to your own self.

On the stage of life, be both actor and audience. Detaching yourself from the roles you play will help you get in touch with the part of you that is not an act.

Real power is not dominance, but spiritual fuel. It is what enables you to perform to your greatest potential.

Because we understand the value of money, we take care not to waste it. If we valued time, energy and positive thoughts, we would likewise economize. The result would be a life full of meaning and purpose.

Giving good wishes to people can produce a positive outcome from even the most negative situation.

Like sunlight, benevolence can filter into the quiet corners of panic in another person's mind and lighten the burden.

If you always understand that the people in your life are there for a reason, you will never be angry.

One who is truly tolerant has no sense of anyone or anything being intolerable.

Despite appearances, people may be doing the best they can. Think that no one is to blame, and the humility in your attitude will enable everyone to move forward.

Judge whether your thoughts, words and actions are beneficial to the scene in which you find yourself. Focusing on your own part is more useful than passing judgment on others.

To seek forgiveness, see yourself with honesty and approach the other with an open heart. Presenting this attitude as a gift will automatically ease the situation.

Brotherhood means understanding that a cry of pain means the same in all languages, and so does a smile.

Sometimes a smile can help someone achieve in a second what would otherwise take a great deal of time.

When love is strong, personalities don't need to impress, for love in itself is impressive and automatically illuminates the important things.

The world is like a hand and its continents like our five fingers. Each finger is different and unique. Yet it is only when they all work together that whatever we put our hand to succeeds.

It is a sign of wisdom to be able to set goals and then, having done so, to let them go. All that is required for success is a vision of the destination. The journey itself will reveal the means that will take you there.

Mistakes will not throw you off course unless you let them stop you. A good navigator keeps a sure eye on the final destination, but steers there through a series of approximations.

Courage is taking a step forward into an area of difficulty without a solution in mind, trusting that whatever help you need will become available.

Spirit

There is in each of us an underground river whose course cannot be daunted. When the surface of life undergoes upheaval, the river changes, flows around, but never dries up. The strong currents that make this river flow are peace, love and spirituality.

Stillness of the spirit does not mean lack of movement. Rather, thoughts and feelings move in the right direction naturally, like a tide pulled by the moon.

The mind that tries to rest only on the surface
of things will be tossed about in every storm.
Dive deeper, to where the peace is.

To feel renewed, take a spiritual holiday. You don't have to go anywhere except inside yourself, away from the obvious.

All human beings have a place inside which is filled with treasures. For some, the space is small. For others, it is a hidden palace.

There is a part of you that is perfect and pure. It is untouched by the less-than-perfect characteristics you have acquired by living in a less-than-perfect world. This part of you is a still and eternal pool. Making time to reach it will bring you untold benefit.

Your physical identity is a world of limited thoughts, feelings and roles. It is quite apart from the being of inner peace and power that is your spiritual personality.

Purifying the soul means putting your highest self in charge. Useless and negative thoughts are removed and annoying habits finished. This is the aim of spiritual study.

Recognizing your spiritual identity is like being reborn.

Truly recognizing God without seeing with physical eyes or knowing with philosophical understanding is to experience a heart link.

The easiest way to meditate on God is to picture him as light shining with love, a being who knows the beginning, the middle and the end of your eternal journey through time, understands everything, and accepts you as you are.

Think of attuning yourself to God as you would turn the dial of a radio, to find a channel without static.

Imagine God as one who sees only the best in you. If you hold yourself to that vision of your own perfection, you will become merciful toward your faults and more easily correct them.

*O*ne basis of self-respect is the faith that someone loves you. Experiencing God's love empowers you to start loving yourself.

When God walks into your life, it is like a laser beam passing across your being. The principal tendency of the light is to restore beauty and value, even if what is visible at first glance is less than beautiful. Meditation is an invitation to light.

Meditation is not complicated. It is simply a means of teaching your mind to think in a different way.

React less, respond more. As you learn to tell your mind what to do, old ways of thinking and doing will change.

As you do, so you become. Every action that you perform is recorded in you, the soul. These imprints ultimately mold your character and destiny. When you understand this principle, you will pay more attention to bringing your best to everything you do.

Through our thoughts we are either gaining power or losing it. Positive thoughts generate power; negative ones waste it.

A clean intellect is like the mind's filter, sorting out thoughts of value from those of waste, enabling you to put into action only the valuable.

When you're engaged in creating something new, the impact of whatever is old is reduced.

If you value your thoughts and use them as carefully as you use money, you will never find yourself spiritually bankrupt.

Learning to talk properly to the self is a spiritual endeavor. When you make a mistake, do you talk lovingly to yourself in your mind, or do you tell yourself off? One habit recognizes your divinity; the other subtly shapes a nature of sorrow.

Make an appointment with yourself at the beginning of each day. When you start with a moment of solitude, even the most crowded of schedules runs more smoothly.

Visualize God as one who is pleased to see you. Then greet others with godly eyes, as if you are meeting long-lost and now-found family. Such good wishes can transform any relationship.

If you are having trouble respecting someone, understand that what you see may be a matter of where the light is falling. Where the sun is not shining may not indicate a gap—only that something is resting in the shadow.

Civilization happens when people see one another with civil eyes.

A relationship is like a tapestry: The fabric is strongest where the threads that hold it together are spun of openness, love and trust.

A racing mind that reacts sensitively to little things indicates thinking that has lost its spiritual strength. Meditation restores that power.

Push yourself like a machine and you will eventually run low on energy. Love your mind by allowing it spaces of silence and it will serve you tirelessly.

*N*otice how your senses are connected to your mind. Anything negative they pick up or generate will disturb the mind's workings. To maintain peace of mind, use your eyes, ears and mouth with care.

True nonviolence is not to hurt anyone even in thought.

Going into silence enables you to manage your thoughts better. You will find there is no need to worry. Most of the answers you are looking for will come to you without too much effort on your part.

Nature has order, happiness and sorrow each in their own time. Knowing that all things move in cycles can give hope that what is uncomfortable now may soon change.

Though the mind often asks for what is visible or material, its needs are deeper and cannot be met by anything superficial or short term. Meditation leads to a meeting point with all that is true and eternal.

Remaining conscious of yourself as a spiritual being while playing your part in the material world requires great detachment.

Freedom means that no one can stop you from doing what is right, or persuade you to do what is wrong.

Perfection is possible or there would be no word for it.

Love of God is to our consciousness like a string to a high-flying kite. When the connection is strong, we are free to rise to any height.

About the Author

Dadi Janki is a woman of wisdom. Her life's journey has been a fulfillment of her early childhood longing to know and come close to God.

Dadi was born in 1916 in India to a devout and philanthropic family. She had no formal education beyond the age of fourteen, her studies being mainly of the scriptures. At the age of twenty-one she joined the Brahma Kumaris World Spiritual University and dedicated her life to the spiritual service of others.

Dadi campaigns for truth and works tirelessly for world peace. She travels worldwide, teaching and sharing her wisdom and deep knowledge of spirituality. She is a soul who refuses to set limits and boundaries as to what is achievable and, in so doing, inspires others to believe that they, too, can make the impossible possible. Recognized worldwide for the depth and insight of her lectures and spiritual classes, her words of wisdom have given wings to countless souls.

Since first arriving in London in 1974, Dadi has overseen the expansion of the Brahma Kumaris' work into more than seventy countries and is now the university's additional administrative head. Dadi is one of the Wisdom Keepers, an eminent group of spiritual leaders convened at United Nations conferences. She is also founder and president of the Janki Foundation for Global Health Care and vice president of the World Congress of Faiths.

About the Brahma Kumaris

The Brahma Kumaris World Spiritual University is an international organization working at all levels of society for positive change. Established in 1937 it now carries out a wide range of educational programs for the development of human and spiritual values throughout its 4,000 centers in over seventy countries.

The University is a non-governmental organization in general consultative status with the Economic and Social Council of the United Nations and in consultative status with UNICEF. It is also the recipient of seven UN Peace Messenger awards.

Locally, centers provide courses and lectures in meditation and positive values, enabling individuals to recognize their true potential and make the most of life.

The University offers all its services free of charge.

BRAHMA KUMARIS WORLD SPIRITUAL UNIVERSITY
INTERNATIONAL HEADQUARTERS

P.O. Box No 2, Mount Abu, Rajasthan 307501, India
Tel: (91) 2974 38261 68 Fax: (91) 2974 38952
E-mail: *bkabu@vsnl.com*

INTERNATIONAL CO-ORDINATING OFFICE & REGIONAL OFFICE FOR EUROPE AND
THE MIDDLE EAST

Global Co-operation House, 65 Pound Lane, London, NW10 2HH, UK
Tel: (44) 181 727 3350 Fax: (44) 181 727 3351
E-mail: *london@bkwsu.com*

AFRICA

Global Museum for a Better World, Maua Close,
off Parklands Road, Westlands, P.O. Box 12349, Nairobi, Kenya
Tel: (254) 2 743 572 Fax: (254) 2 743 885
E-mail: *bkwsugm@holidaybazaar.com*

AUSTRALIA AND EAST ASIA
78 Alt Street, Ashfield, Sydney, NSW 2131, Australia
Tel: (+61) 2 9716 7066 Fax: (+61) 2 9716 7795
E-mail: *indra@one.net.au*

NORTH AND SOUTH AMERICAS AND THE CARIBBEAN
Global Harmony House, 46 S. Middle Neck Road
Great Neck, NY 11021, USA
Tel: (+1) 516 773 0971 Fax: (+1) 516 773 0976
E-mail: *newyork@bkwsu.com*

RUSSIA AND CIS
Angels' House 2, Gospitalnaya Sq., Build 1, Moscow 111020, Russia
Tel: (+7) 095 263 02 47 Fax: (+7) 095 261 32 24
E-mail: *bksu@glasnet.ru*
http://*www.bkwsu.com*

Main Centers
United Kingdom and Ireland

Global Co-operation House
65 Pound Lane,
London, England NW10 2HH
Tel: 0181 727 3350
E-mail: *london@bkwsu.com*

Global Retreat Center, Nuneham Park
Nuneham Courtenay
Oxford, OX44 9PG
Tel: 01865 343 551
E-mail: *infoshare@bkwsugrc.demon.co.uk*

8 Haxby Court, Felbridge Close
Atlantic Wharfe
Cardiff, Wales CFI 5BH
Tel: 1222 480 557

20 Polwarth Crescent
Edinburgh, Scotland EHI 1 IHW
Tel: 0131 229 7220
E-mail: *bkedinburgh@compuserve.com*

36 Lansdowne Road, Ballsbridge
Dublin 4, Ireland
Tel: (+353) 1 660 3967
E-mail: *bknick@indigo.ie*

North and South Americas

The United States:
1821 Beacon St.
Brookline, MA 02445
Tel: 1-617-734-1464
E-mail: *boston@bkwsu.com*

1101 Grove St. #5B
^hicago, IL 60201
: 1-847-733-1232
ail: *pratima@compuserve.com*

1 E. Manoa Rd.
ɔnolulu, HI 96822
Tel: 1-808-988-3141
E-mail: *hawaii@bkwsu.com*

1200 North June St.
Apt. 410
Los Angeles, CA 90038
Tel: 1-323-461-8028
E-mail: *maglstblues@usa.net*

The Meditation Centre and Gallery
306 Fifth Ave., 2nd Floor
New York, NY 10001
Tel: 1-212-564-9533

4160 S.W. 4th St.
Miami, FL 33134
Tel: 1-305-442-2252
E-mail: *miami@bkwsu.com*

710 Marquis
San Antonio, TX 78216
Tel: 1-210-344-8343
E-mail: *texas@bkwsu.com*

North and South Americas

401 Baker St.
San Francisco, CA 94117
Tel: 1-415-563-4459
E-mail: *bksfo@aol.com*

302 Sixteenth St.
Seal Beach, CA 90740
Tel: 1-562-430-4711
E-mail: *dianetil@pacbell.net*

Mind's Eye Museum
2207 E. Busch Blvd.
Tampa, FL 33612
Tel: 1-813-935-0736
E-mail: *tampa@bkwsu.com*

Canada:
897 College St.
Toronto, Ontario M6H 1A1
Tel: 1-416-537-3034
E-mail: *bktoronto@titan.ten.net*

Trinidad:

55-57 Pointe-A-Pierre Rd.
San Fernando Trinidad and Tobago
Tel: 1-809-653-9642
E-mail: *rajayoga@trinidad.net*